Swastika into Lotus

Books by Richard Katrovas

Green Dragons (1983)
Snug Harbor (1986)
The Public Mirror (1990)
The Book of Complaints (1993)
Prague, USA (1996)
Dithyrambs (1998)
Mystic Pig (2001, 2008)
The Republic of Burma Shave (2001)
Prague Winter (2005)
The Years of Smashing Bricks: An Anecdotal Memoir (2007)
Scorpio Rising: Selected Poems (2011)
Raising Girls in Bohemia: Meditations of an American Father: A Memoir in Essays (2014)

Edited by Richard Katrovas

Ten Years After the Velvet Revolution: Voices from the Czech Republic

Swastika into Lotus

Richard Katrovas

Carnegie Mellon University Press
Pittsburgh 2016

Acknowledgments

Some of these poems appeared in *The American Literary Review,*
Crazyhorse, Cutthroat: a Journal of the Arts, New Orleans on New Orleans,
and *North American Review.*

Book design by Jackie Sipe

Library of Congress Control Number 2015945713
ISBN 978-0-88748-608-1
Printed and bound in the United States of America

10 9 8 7 6 5 4 3 2 1

for Krista, without whom poetry would be dead to my heart

Contents

Courting the Succubus, His Muse || 9
Ella Gone || 10
Essay on Poetry and Poetry Readings || 12
My Daughter's Beauty || 13
Ancient Aliens || 15
Elevator Music || 17
"American Football" || 18
Mistress || 19
Second Anniversary || 21
Carolyn || 22
The Night and Day Café || 23
Essay on Teaching || 24
Essay on Fucking || 25
Terminal Velocity || 26

Two Dithyrambs
   The Blight || 30
   The Dogs || 37

A Valentine for Krista || 43
"How's it Tasting?" || 44
A Topical Bestiary of 2010 || 45
April 18, 2011 || 49
Cash Washes Up on Japanese Shores || 50

Courting the Succubus, His Muse

The gourd is full of milk and blood.
He bears it to her with both hands
And sets it down upon the wood.
She sits in silence as he stands
Expectant, hungry for assent.
The midday moon is paper-thin.
A blast of chill stirs up a rent
In shade that closes, dark, again.
She stares beyond him, to that place
Where trees are hissing like the swans
She slaughtered in her youth. Her face
Is almost beautiful, though wan.
He knows that she will never love,
That she will only fuck wild things
And no mere man is wild enough,
Despite the stories that she brings
Her perfect body to men's dreams
To drain them clean of energy.
Beyond the garden horseshit steams
In golden piles where beasts romp free.
He begs her with his eyes to take
Him in, to let him be her man
For love's if not misery's sake.
Her eyes glow red. Her black wings fan
Redolent as she sighs, demurs
So faintly with a fluttering blink.
Such concupiscent fools she lures
For sport, whether or not she'll drink.

Ella Gone

Born into a broken marriage, she still
Scrawls smiling, intact families, and wonders
What it's like to live with parents in one place.
My baby holds all goodness in her face.
The quiet of her room is claps of thunder,
Her absences are unremitting chill.

Six years to my fifty-seven, my girl
Presumes a permanence I cultivate,
Though when she's six and thirty I'll be dead.
If somewhere's a nowhere that begs to be fed
All sentimental loss is child of fate.
Our portioned times together will unfurl

From that blossom which is the fact she lives
And that we willed her into being despite
The suffocating sadness of our bond.
Of spicy foods and boys she is not fond.
I spoil her lavishly so that she might,
When she's a world away from here, derive

A little pleasure from her memory
Of fatherly indulgences and joy
In routine simple things of our homelife.
Today she told me on the phone of strife
With older sister, and coveted toy.
As she chattered I felt the storied Tree

Of Life explode beneath my father heart.
I felt each one of the thousands of miles
Between her vibrancy and my decay.
And yet I felt so thankful for each day

Alone with my new wife, or walking aisles
Of stores unharried by Ella's canny, smart

Acquisitive eye for gaudy, worthless stuff.
Each year I'll wait my turn with that odd mix
Of loss and joy, the wounding paradox
That hangs suspended over dreams and shocks
Awake the fading, other self to fix
With frozen stare what never is enough.

Essay on Poetry and Poetry Readings

As long as fourteen-year-old boys and girls
Hide poems of love beneath their underwear
And socks, so this dead art will prattle on.
By "dead" I mean arcane beyond mere purpose;
By "purpose" I mean that sometimes even church
Is entertaining to a nonbeliever,
Especially when the homily
Is abstract meditation on free will.
When poems enshrine such magical thinking
As children, saints and field commanders feed
Contrary voices in their dreaming heads,
It is poison to the body politic,
But in the sense of chemotherapy.

Yet if I see another idiot mount
A stage and enter the state of tainted grace
That is the dismal ego swamp of love
Of one's own voice, if I must suffer one
More fool who cannot check his fucking watch
Because his head is too far up his ass
Exploring diadems of earthly wonder,
I shall rise, depart as loudly as I can,
Leaving in my wake a cankerous disdain
For all who swill at the trough of beauty.

My Daughter's Beauty

Fifteen, 5'9", exotically beautiful
By any standard, my blond Annie lives
To paint her face and wiggle into clothes
Too stylishly revealing for a child.
When she promenades on Wenceslas Square
Grown men gawk and even women turn their heads.
I, her father, am mortified, resist
The urge to slap the hell out of some forty-
Something Slavic ass undressing her with
His stare. I simply cannot win the fight
With her; I cannot order her to be
A child, present her childish self in Prague
When all the other girls are likewise
Exhibitionists of sexuality
they mimic from movies, TV, billboards,
slick magazines and music videos.
She feels a power in her appearance that
Is real, but leering danger is also real,
Though greatest danger is to lose herself
Reflected in the eyes of someone else
Than who she'll be when heads no longer turn.
Sometimes, through all that make-up and posturing
Are glimpses of a woman I'd like to know,
Someone powerful and compassionate,
Someone who sees the world and not herself
Reflected in its shining surfaces.
All fathers of such beauty know despair
That shades to resignation, then to wonder.
Her face and body—and that bifurcation
Is symptom of her status as a thing—
Are currency that crosses every border
Except the ones into such realms where women

And girls are chattel still, are covered up,
Their bodies rendered unavailable
Especially to themselves in public spheres.
My darling woman-girl, my tall, blond beauty
Goes forth with confidence upon Prague's streets
Not yet caring (much) what men and women see,
Caring mainly that she's there with resonance,
Reveling in the power of her mere presence.

Ancient Aliens

I'll watch this shit for hours on History Channel
While grading papers and tapping e-mail drone.
A coterie of hucksters makes its case
That ET helped to build the pyramids,
Rendering megatons of granite weightless.
The geoglyphs of Peru are evidence
Of prehistoric crosshatched airport runways,
As though traversing light years might require
The same mechanics as a DC 10.
As a kid I inhaled *Chariots of the Gods*
And wanted to believe von Däniken
Was not humping my celestial leg.
I was fifteen, living with a family
I did not know in Sasebo, Japan.
My zits seemed neon phosphorescent, boner
Irrepressible as summer starlight.
Of course the aliens came to earth and gave
Up secrets to technologies that led
Us earthlings out of Neolithic darkness
Right into Wanda Whackman's glorious drawers,
Or to that night I kissed a beautiful girl
On the bus ride back from Nagasaki
And touched her everywhere but in her heart.
What can be more alien on this planet
Than a fifteen-year-old American boy
Among the Japanese, just twenty-three years
After we'd nuked them into our own image?
What's more alien than teenage Americans
Whose fathers patrolled the coasts of Vietnam
In 1968, whose mothers patrolled
The dining rooms of the Officers' Club
Below the Quonset huts of Dragon Heights?

Who moved those stones at Stonehenge? Who moved those stones
On Easter Island? Who carved those Nazca Lines
Into figures only discernible from
The sky? Girls and boys prodded by old men
In their thirties and forties, old men scared
Of death and hearing voices on the wind.

Elevator Music

So, I'm dead, and that Christian tripe is true.
There is a hell and I am in it for
The mother of all Long Hauls, the Big Rue.
Oh, that I had hedged my bet, settled more
On inching toward if not leaping into faith,
I'd not be shuffling here, holding this ticket,
Awaiting the Big Push, then forever to bathe
In white flames fueled by all that's wicked.
I killed no one, caused very little pain.
Incredulity was my only sin.
Such faith as buys one bliss is quite insane.
The game is rigged; too many idiots win.
As I inch forward in this queue of doom,
I hear a hearty farting from the gloom.

"American Football"

That I would even use the phrase suggests
A false yet useful worldliness, a scope
Far greater than my caste would indicate.
The phrase signals, "I've lived abroad! I've watched
The Premier League in European pubs!"
In fact I hate the game; its ethos rests
On boring strategies and rules that *cope*,
Merely, with competition's link to fate,
How luck and skill dovetail in every botched
Clear kick on goal, and every header rubs

Against the grain of what is beautiful
In sport, at least to my Yankee Doodle eyes.
Give me smashmouth football over soccer.
Give me concussions, shattered bones, ripped muscles,
Strategies of season-long attrition.
Give me huge men heaving their bountiful
Frames against each other with such grace that size
Seems incidental to the role of stalker
Of fleet backs and fleeter ends, men who bustle
Along the line of scrimmage on a mission.

A hundred and sixty-pound defensive end,
I was the scourge of JV quarterbacks.
I blitzed on every down, so spent the game
With most the action at my back; the coach
Didn't seem to care; he was drunk on power
And vodka, said my job was to defend
Right flank from sweeps and register some sacks.
Helter skelter, I dreamed of gridiron fame.
Much less than mediocre, I could not broach
The fact of pain, the realm where bruises flower.

Mistress

Your bedroom, fire-red and girly, bore
Our secret for a decade and a half.
My Ema's New Orleans aunt and model
For how a woman lives alone in style,
You witnessed my oldest daughter's blossoming.
Those nights I informed you, lying in the dark,
My wife was pregnant with yet another girl,
You wept convulsively, but when you stopped
It seemed as though you really didn't care.
Condition of our friendship was quite clear.
Ours was classic circumstance; we had our cake
And ate it, you your freedom, I family.

Living on two continents, convenience
A factor in our bond, I rented space,
Those months I had to schlep across Big Nasty,
In your cramped attic where three of seven cats
Would grace the bed and chairs I never used.
Those times my wife would visit, to fetch a thing
We stored in attic walls, her allergies
Were so violent she wore white doctors' masks.
When I'd return to Prague, the cat hair on
My bags would send her, swollen, to the clinic.

I never want to live a lie again,
Though what mendacity our bond required
Was sweetest subterfuge I'll not regret.
You were the truest friend and loyal companion.
Dear Susan, whom I'll never see again,
Whose sultry voice is heavy as the air
On Uptown summer nights before a storm,
And silent to my life forever more,

I hope the city that you love so well,
Whose destruction sent you into mourning,
And for which you will always be for me
Its quiet, elegant embodiment,
Is faithful to your faithful love of it.
I hope contentment wraps you in her arms.

Second Anniversary

A two-time loser, I learned my lesson well:
My life would be a singularity.
Past fifty, all romance is a crystal bell
That shatters when shaken with alacrity.
And yet, when you appeared like sudden light
All cynicism scurried forth and fled
The rotting space that was my false delight
In every intimate lie I've ever said.
Wed to you, my darling, I'm wed to truth.
You are a sweetness more profound than those
Confections youthful romance feeds the uncouth
Narcissistic heart in its hormonal throes.
You are the only woman in the world
When in my arms your naked body's curled.

Carolyn

Ambition and beauty such as you owned
Seemed wasted on the world of poetry.
Charisma oozing from your presence stoned
My boyish confidence, quite pummeled me.
Carolyn, what we were was *très* absurd,
And yet I would not change the past to suit
My pride's pained recall; I would not change a word
Exchanged with you, even when you tried to shoot
Me with a pellet gun as I turned to leave.
Verlaine and Rimbaud we were not, even though
We were almost as kinky to believe
That words and flesh into each other flow.
The flawed goddess of my ignorant youth,
You giddily dissembled unto truth.

The Night and Day Café

Ten fixed stools along an L-shaped counter,
It was safe harbor for the teenaged spawn
Of beach-town haciendas and perfect lawns.
Sixty cents for three eggs, toast, hash browns, water,
Economy of scale determined we
Would keep the small joint rocking year-round profit.
Through Window Pane and 'shrooms we all saw fit
To congregate and fry in our ennui
Until hallucinations drove us home
Or back to moonlit beach to smoke a bowl
Of hash and fuck and talk as tides would roll
And thoughts become as curls of hissing foam.
Neither priestess nor mother, the fry cook fed
The narcissistic joy we, sadly, would shed.

Essay on Teaching

Now older than their parents, I despair
When pop culture reference evokes blank stare.
I make nameplates on construction paper
And require they display them all semester.
On Rate My Professor I have ten hits:
Five say I'm grand and five that I'm the pits.
Towards pretty ones I once would try to charm
I'm neither solicitous nor falsely warm.
Though no longer fighting grade inflation,
My frank critiques entitled hearts still stun.
Where once I brimmed with prideful certainty,
Before a classroom now my doubts prod me
Through circumlocutions as dense as sludge.
I sing in minor key of useful knowledge.

Essay on Fucking

In early '70s my college life
Was fraught with joyful promiscuity
Of a pretty boy. My fickle heart was rife
With less than crystal-clear acuity.
My "life" and "heart" were strangers in the night,
Like Frank Sinatra and Peter Frampton.
The future spread its legs, though was not bright,
For I was neither hung nor Fortune's son.
My life I measured by each casual kiss.
I fingered my poor prospects, made them squeal
And moan until each greedy one knew bliss.
I fucked my fear until I could not feel.
Oh, Youth, you are the Saint of Sticky Thighs.
Each blistered tongue invokes you as it dies.

Terminal Velocity

Black-robed, stationed behind her cluttered desk,
Harry Connick Jr.'s mother married us
St. Patrick's Day near '80 Vieux Carré.
Coming down from acid, we bore the risk
Of freaking out at some imagined menace,
Though sadness stalking us we could not see.

A friendship worthy of a marriage bloomed,
Though secrets scurried in the dark like roaches.
I was as faithful as an alley cat.
You lied that we'd have kids; our bond was doomed
As toddler in a crib with gas and matches.
The troll beneath our bridge grew gray and fat.

Brutality you suffered before we wed
You binged to douse the memory of, and danced
And drank, off nights, at Rampart drag queen shows
With your gay posse, then threw up in our bed.
Your stunning youthful beauty smashed against
The sickening nightmare of survivor's woes.

Dance finally saved you from a broken heart.
Indeed, ballet was marvelous medicine.
But in your early thirties you were too old
To make the corps with sparrow girls as smart
As mildew but blithe and malleable, thin.
Your solid woman's body was too bold.

Your triumph was the daily grind of work
At bar before the mirrors and the tap
Tap tapping of your Serbian maestro's stick,
Self-satisfaction of his Slavic smirk.

One day I felt the lie in my heart snap.
I transformed from clueless chump to cynic.

I was patron of an art I did not love.
I subsidized your sweaty dream long past
The point adult perception should believe
That practice *sans* performance is enough.
Our precarious balance could not last.
You did not love me until I turned to leave.

Two Dithyrambs

Perhaps for all the wrong reasons, I am enchanted by the choral ejaculations of Attic tragedy, and am fascinated by the question of how tragic drama, the likes of which developed nowhere else on earth, issued from a particular moment in ancient history, the product of satyr plays, dithyrambs, and epics. As far as I can tell, what fragments of dithyrambs we have are not necessarily representative of those immediate precursors of Aeschylus's Oresteia, *and I imagine that one must look directly into Aeschylian drama to see the vestiges of dithyrambs in their latest development, a period when they were original compositions and not simply received, folkish forms. My dithyrambs are highly stylized blank verse monologues framed by choral outbursts. In both of these poems, several dialectics are at play, not the least of which is a simultaneous yearning for, and parody of, a "high" lyric style.*

—RK

The Blight

Female Chorus:
The blight will husband nescient woe, and feed
An idiot's laughter to a burning wind.

Male Chorus:
The blight will be a scourge of wonder, scourge
Of laughter on a burning wind, and on
The tongue of one

Female Chorus:
                              Who burns from ear to ear.

Male and Female Chorus:
To know the blight is on [his] [her] own dim life.

Female Chorus Leader:
Dim room, light laughter, sparkling conversation

Male Chorus Leader:
The bill for just the liquor will exceed
What all the tuxedoed bleach-toothed waiters here
Will glean from lipoed patrons in a season.

Female Chorus:
When vermin riot on the wind, contest
The quiet of the field in frenzied flight

Male Chorus:
Abundant blessings turn, as rot is such
A turning,

Female Chorus:
                    Upon themselves, and so upon

Female and Male Chorus:
The press of time fermenting in the eyes
Of statues, mothers, solitary men.

Female Chorus Leader:
Each bulging crotch presages story lines
As stale and thin as weather on a jet.
They circle now the smorgasbord and bars
Of this garish pit, this felt-lined banquet hall
On west Van Ness, a hotel on the make
To earn a third star in the Mobil Guide.
And the Talent's here with cloying agents,
And all the dolls of flesh the Talent must
Perform upon, and all the cameramen,
Sound engineers, Best Boys and grips and those,
Of course, who lead them all, the little men
With weasel eyes who call themselves producers,
Directors: merchants of the dreams men dream
While grunting weekly on abstracted wives,
Or pumping squint-eyed over toilet bowls.

Female Chorus:
Praise all who pray mechanically, praise all
Whose prayers are swirls of pearl flushed Heavenward.

Male Chorus:
Praise dirty deeds that roil in dirty words.

Male Chorus Leader:
Ten years ago she was the best, a whore
Or Catholic schoolgirl, office mouse or goddess
With a whip, in cheesy leather, or chiffon,
Her range, within the genre, was dazzling.
But then she got the notion she could act,
Tried art films for a while, the kinky kind
That make professors want to masturbate
And publish articles no one can read.
Poor thing, she plunged from such a bliss, and so
The *Beast with Two Backs* honors her tonight.
Whoever said this industry is heartless?

Female Chorus:
Caress the air and call it dancing; caress
The dark and call it terror of extinction.

Male Chorus:
Caress the brow of someone slumping deathward.

Female Chorus:
Caress yourself and weep that such compassion
Is like a gentle rain upon the sea.

Female Chorus Leader:
I'm only forty, pass for thirty-four,
And yet tonight the heavies gathered here
To deal out statuettes—a golden shaft
It's said is actual cast of someone I
Once worked with, on and under—honor me
For a Lifetime of Achievement, as though
The sixty-seven titles that bear my name

May constitute legitimate career.
I'm here to see old friends, a cameraman
I loved for several weeks, a makeup girl
I loved a little longer, my first co-star,
A withered bull so dulled by gin he now
Directs a show for kids on Public Access.
All work is only work in the great grind
Of days, all passion faked on the wheel of dull
And dulling wakeful hours, the blight of hours,
The blight of days, each crossed and counted off
Toward nothing, or toward a Golden Phallus
For a Lifetime of Achievement, spreading wide
For all the talent of the industry,
Achieving control of gag reflex, of what
A body weeps to know about itself.
Yet I have known as well the joy of art,
For I was Nora once in summer stock.

Male Chorus:
The blight of days is ferried on the wind.

Female Chorus:
The blightful wind is kiss upon the air.

Male Chorus Leader:
She plays the room, drink in hand, pausing now
To chat with several ancient grips who've watched
Her under bright lights take a puzzled pony,
Accommodate, indeed, anyone or thing
The story or director fancied she
Should take; for she's a trooper, true-blue pro.

Female Chorus:
So many tiny mouths upon the land

Male Chorus:
So many hungry heads aswarm, the sky
Is shaded toward the dusk at height of day

Female Chorus:
Praise the woman banging pans and screaming.
Praise voices railing out against the blight.

Male Chorus:
Praise fools who seek to shoo away disaster.

Male Chorus Leader:
The white-gloved waiters balance trays of drinks,
Spot the power in the room and play to it,
For they are pretty boys who will be stars
Someday, as someday everyone must star
In the story of his passing from the world.
Though some, before the final scene is shot,
Before the money shot is in the can,
Will know the honor of their peers, will stand
Upon a stage and hear old friends applaud
As though each one could drive away despair,
Each one were standing at a field's edge clapping,
Banging pans to drive away a menace
That's unaffected, wholly unimpressed.

Female Chorus Leader:
A waiter spilled a vodka gimlet down
The purchased cleavage of Pricilla Star,

And Peter Lancelot, her eunuch date,
Himself a not-so-secret fancier
Of boys, feigned umbrage, with a little smile.
Now as the bright lights of the industry
Tuck into Abalone a la King
Washed down with Napa Valley chardonnay,
The dwarf Hugh Hefty, sweet freak of comical
Proportions, star of *Biggest Little Man*,
Is weeping on the knee of Princess Pie.
His wife has left him for a younger man.

Male Chorus:
Praise garish sparkle of fake pieties.

Female Chorus:
Praise her who dreams beyond demeaning acts.

Male Chorus:
Praise all who dream beyond demeaning lives.
Praise dreams that shelter us from daily blight.

Male Chorus Leader:
Once queen of Triple X, she mounts the stage
In olive pantsuit, modestly made-up,
As though we honor her for selling dish soap,
Or opening new markets overseas
For some innocuous gadget in the house.

Female and Male Chorus:
Bless blighted hearts that burn with dignity.

Male Chorus Leader:
As she, who once was caricature of
Desire, speaks too close to the microphone
And sends electric shrieks throughout the room,
She doesn't pause but speaks across the spine-
Plucking noise of a cheap sound system, thanks,
It seems with little irony, her mother,
Her agent dead now for a dozen years,
And everyone who ever loved her well.

The Dogs

Female Chorus:
When something ugly's brewing in the Gulf

Male Chorus:
When ugly weather turns so dangerous
The smart ones flee the coast for higher ground

Female Chorus:
As wind becomes a danger to us all
And water rises to the window ledge

Male Chorus:
As death becomes a dark and soaking rain

Female Chorus:
Approaching as a vast contingency

Male Chorus:
First veering east

Female Chorus:
                    Then wheeling to the west

Male and Female Chorus:
Then seeming to take aim on all you know

Male Chorus:
Illusions tethered to the flesh explode.

Younger Female Chorus Leader:
My love is such a coward under all
His charming bluster, a man whose fear of dark,

37

Of what he cannot beat upon or steer,
Is constant calculation of his days.
His exhibitions of aggression seem
Such calculated risks as cowards take.
And yet I love him for his blustering.

Female Chorus:
Praise her who knows the truth and loves the lie.

Older Female Chorus Leader:
He left her to this killer storm, tore out
As first hard winds ripped fronds and whipped high wires.
He screeched his wheels on pavement soaked, she said
Before the lines went down, before the old
Were hustled from their living spaces, propped
In this elementary school gymnasium,
Before I, old mother, neighborhood witch,
Could go to her, my only child, woman
Too good for such as he, too good, too good.
So good she would not leave without her dogs,
Four hulking shepherds she has loved as men
Have come and gone, four dogs who would not fit
In either car, or even both since his
Was loaded down with baubles, stuff, and she
Would not take one or two, would only go
If all her darlings left with her, so now,
As babies howl and adolescents preen,
As neighbors white and black are forced to stand
Upon a common ground of shared disaster,
As roar of wind reverberates and rain
Becomes a solid thing against these walls,

My terror is for her who would not leave
Her dogs for any man or fear of death.

Female Chorus:
Praise clarity of violent death foreseen.

Male Chorus:
Praise clarity of violent death foreseen.

Female Chorus:
Praise wind that is the breath of godless hope.

Male Chorus:
Praise sheeted rain that is the face of God.

Younger Female Chorus Leader:
My darlings whimper, bellies pressed to floor.
They feel how soon the roof will go, and doom
Will pour upon us from eternity
To wash away all fictions of desire.
Or they feel nothing but confusion, feel,
In the tender knot of their beings, shades
Of undulating nothing, death's greeting.

Female Chorus:
The weather of the heart is nothingness.
The weather of the heart is therefore changeless.

Male Chorus:
The peace before the ravaging of wind
Is death on haunches waiting for its time.

Younger Female Chorus Leader:
We packed both cars but lightly, yet then we saw
That, even as we unpacked everything
But what he thought essential, our tiny cars,
Our testimonies to good stewardship,
Would not accommodate four hulking hounds.
I said he'd simply have to unpack more.
He said I'd have to choose which dog to leave.
I kissed him on the cheek and said goodbye.
Now Category Five, with silly name
Like Chip or Chet or Chuck, will heave the lake
Across the city toward the river, destroy
More property than small atomic blast,
And any second I will lose my roof.
I am a martyr to my love of dogs,
Or simply to a man who'd leave me here
To die with whining dogs curled at my feet.

Male Chorus:
The prudent heart will live to love again.

Female Chorus:
The prudent heart has never loved before.

Older Female Chorus Leader:
A childless woman at midlife, my child
Is beautiful the way a woman is
When beauty skims against the grain of time.
Twice pregnant, twice she sacrificed a child
To promises that men would leave their wives.
This latest one was free and clear, though dumb
As fungus, and hadn't held a job in years.

40

So now, with credit card he stole from her,
He holes up in a Comfort Inn in Mobile,
And she awaits her death inside her house
With eight months left to pay the mortgage off.

Male Chorus:
Beware the calm of solitary life.

Female Chorus:
Embrace the calm of solitary life.

Older Female Chorus Leader:
What if this high-ground cement structure gave
To savage wind and crushed us all? So what?
I've lived one life in turmoil, another one,
Or half at least, in twilight of old age,
Alone, but for the television's glow.
She visits twice a week, though her house lay
But eight blocks down the boulevard from mine,
A brisk walk for one still young, or almost young.

Female Chorus:
Beware the love of one in love with death.

Male Chorus:
Beware unspoken loss, unburied grief.

Older Female Chorus Leader:
As rage of wind becomes protracted roar
And every brow is stitched along the seam
Of woe and wonder, the candlelight is sweet

Upon the smallest faces looking up
With mouths agape, as if to greet a god.

Male Chorus:
Praise the brutal wind that takes us quickly.

Female Chorus:
Praise brutal births that are the gates to life.

Younger Female Chorus Leader:
His hat that hung upon a peg when he
Was home from work; his pipe that stank so sweetly;
His arms, his lap, his voice like summer breeze;
His silence Sunday afternoons, his sadness
In the evenings when he drank his whiskey.
Then monster of his absence ate our lives.
Oh father, quiet man with gentle eyes,
Are you this pause, or what will follow soon?

A Valentine for Krista

February 14, 2010

We are the stuff of stars exploding still
From that event horizon of no time.
When we embrace all empty spaces fill
With light, and silence spews a holy chime.
The sky extends forever, and yet must end
When everything collapses on itself,
At which moment even our dust will rend
From dust to settle upon the temporal shelf
Of nothingness, or all that God will be
When nothing carries being in its heart.
I found you as one foundering at sea
Beholds an island, feels despair depart.
As true love is timeless, I will love you past
All endings and beginnings, where all will last.

"How's it Tasting?"

I wore tuxedos through the early '80s
In four-star Vieux Carré posh eateries.
I was a charming fraud who kept two lies
Ahead of haughty clients' jaundiced eyes.
I faked sophistication about wines,
Kept perky and chatty snorting white lines.
My evil maître d' skimmed off my tips.
My evil chef threatened to grill my lips.
A disquieting anti-*esprit de corps*
Greeted all who sauntered through the service door.
And yet I miss that time of my late youth,
The sexy afterhours of life uncouth.
Table to table, I measured out my days
In gratuities and funky, casual lays.

When I moved my family into Midwest snow
Eight years, six months, two weeks, three days ago,
Small-town "fine dining" was rendered something quaint.
"How's it tasting?" all manic waitstaff bleat,
Crawling across my palate and my tongue.
"Get out of my mouth!" I jokingly have sung.
Their puzzlement is that of scolded dogs
That tilt adorable heads in doggy fogs.
Sometimes I give a nuanced, honest answer,
As though explaining progress of a cancer.
Ye ol' egocentric predicament
Is bitter aftertaste of all that's meant
In honest explanations of our pleasure.
We taste the bile of loss in all we measure.

A Topical Bestiary of 2010

Glenn Beck
The next door neighbors' yapping beast
Was unrelenting as the tide.
We celebrated when it died.
We didn't mourn it in the least,
Until the quiet was a hymn
To all the nonsense of the world,
The dangerous lies that get unfurled
Before our senses rendered dim
By ambient noise of idiots,
And dogs and cars and dripping spigots.

Michele Bachmann
A tiny lizard scared my girl,
As it darted from a heating vent.
Not four, she screeched and stamped and sent
The poor thing up a wall to hurl
Itself against the windowpane.
The sun was bright, the breezes thin,
My drama princess calm within
Her wonderment at how I strained
To trap the culprit of her fear.
I hauled it by its tail with care.

Carl Rove
A polar bear will eat her cub
When seals and walruses are scarce.
Such brutal logic makes for fierce
Assessments of the human club:
The body politic we feed
Such lies as roil all hateful hearts.
Defilement ends as passion starts

Its trek across the wastes of need.
A bloody snout and mother's eyes
Are antidote to bloody lies.

George W. Bush
In roadkill cookbooks freshness counts
Much more than butchering technique.
All flesh in desert heat will stink
Within an hour of its bounce
Across the acrid burning tar.
Behold the ruptured armadillo
Decaying in its shell of woe!
The sides of roads its corpses mar
Each desolate, monotonous mile
Of our nation's vacuous smile.

Donald Rumsfeld
To this day my wife is traumatized
By having squashed a running bird.
Her ex, a magnificent turd,
Had bullied her, had fantasized
The car would miss the thousands flocked
Upon the road to Kennesaw.
One runner fell into doom's maw.
She drove for hours, mildly shocked,
The shit beside her holding forth
On wildlife's gross extrinsic worth.

Rush Limbaugh
Youngest brother hosted tapeworm
That kept him sick for weeks on end.
We called the thing his "special friend."

46

We heckled anyone infirm.
They killed the beast with Praziquantel.
We fished it from the toilet bowl
And kept it in a jar we stole
From neighbor's mother's windowsill.
My kid brother would proudly show
That intimacy few can know.

Sarah Palin
I had regular sex with one
Whose rhesus monkey hated me.
Chained to its fake Joshua tree
It screeched and backflipped at our fun.
The little bastard bit me twice
And strained to rip my flesh each night
Mama and I took carnal flight.
I taunted it, and was not nice.
But when the little pisser died,
I took a lonely, mournful ride.

Rand Paul
My ex-wife's mother's quiet man
Each birthday roasted full-grown pig.
We turned it in a makeshift rig
He'd fashioned from an old oilcan.
A Czech dude through and through,
He drank Slivovitz for breakfast
And was a connoisseur of rest.
Prince of Leisure, each breath he drew
Was testament to *laissez-faire*.
His pig, our joy, was free of care.

Dick Cheney

Those summers driving, windows down,
The dead skunk every hundred miles
Would leave us gasping in kid piles
On Chrysler backseats; our dad's frown
Would turn to threats of violence.
"It's only death!" he'd shout, then swig
His whisky, fire up a cig.
Our mother straddled every fence
Within the sickness that was *we*,
The deadened longings that was she.

Roger Ailes

Some punk spray-painted swastika—
That symbol of a strutting doom
Against the grain of chanted *om*—
On east wall of Sunrise Yoga.
My yogini wife was saddened,
but changed it to a yellow lotus:
Ganesha will unburden us
When ugly ones their vile thoughts send
(Such chains of sorrow's bleak decree)
To those blessed ones whose hearts are free.

April 18, 2011

It is snowing in southwest Michigan.
Such weather is unusual so late.
The trees are squirting buds that advocate
For green profusions that yesterday began
To grunt and poke and strain toward full-blown spring.
Now fleeced, the trees are January stark.
Though clocks, sprung forward, hedge against the dark,
We hear the arias our miseries sing
When darkness is a salve to all that white.
If global warming is the fangs of doom
I see its poison wafting, from this room.
The future will be mottled if not bright.
Perhaps I'll die before the killing trend.
I hear my children's voices on this wind.

Cash Washes Up on Japanese Shores

*Safes are washing up along the tsunami-battered coast, and police
are trying to find their owners—a unique problem in a country
where many people, especially the elderly, still stash their cash at
home. By one estimate, some $350 billion worth of yen doesn't
circulate.*

—AP

1.

Fourteen, 6'1", a hundred and thirty pounds,
I heisted cash from my stepmother's drawer.
That she'd not miss fifty thousand astounds
Me now; for even though we were not poor
We were seven living on lieutenant's pay.
Three hundred and sixty yen to each greenback:
I was filthy rich for one long summer day
In Sasebo, Japan, ward of a "West Pac
Widow" whose husband haunted the coast of war.
What will a boy with so much money do?
He'll slouch downtown and slink into a bar
Where hardened women wait for night and rue
Departures of the ships they service well.
He'll pay for that from which all riches swell.

2.

"99 Islands"
We rented boats from Special Services
And motored to an archipelago
Where boys could smoke and drink and flaunt their vices
At seabirds, lizards, rodents, bats that stow
Their wild lives in granite caves the army used
For anti-aircraft guns in World War Two.
Graffiti scratched in kanji had infused,
No doubt, sketches of vaginas with the true

50

Ignoble beauty of a young man's fear.
Glimpsing the sky, they filled their idle hours
Meditating on the source of all desire,
The velvet foil of all men's brutal powers.
A flash, but thirty miles from where they drew
Their cartoon dreams of bliss, cooked a human stew.

3.

"Atrocity Museum"
Sixteen, a summer tour bus guide, I read
Hersey's *Hiroshima* in preparation
For a visit to a marker of the dead,
The museum at ground zero, bastion
Of Nagasaki's legacy of horror.
An ancient woman in kimono stood
Stock-still and stared into the mirror
A glass case became in lamplight; the wood
Within, a tiny cradle, was charred black
But otherwise pristine; she did not blink,
It seemed, for twenty minutes, and the lack
Of emotion in her face seemed the brink
Of human understanding of all pain,
The limit of what we may, in truth, call sane.

4.

The 1969 Kyushu Karate Tournament
The five hundred packing the bleachers would roar
At each clean point; my feet and hands were hot,
Quick as whips, and it seemed that I could score
On anyone, that I would have a shot

At winning the Kyushu tournament.
My semifinal was against a guy
Renowned for a killer's temperament.
He smirked as he bowed, then looked me in the eye.
Ten years older, muscled up, his calloused hands
And feet could smash through tempered wooden walls.
As we bowed a murmur wafted through the stands.
But I attacked, a maladroit beast that mauls
For sheer joy in rage, sheer power vented.
He kicked me in the balls and forfeited.

5.
I cannot think of "dignity" and not
Recall the faces of the people there.
Young, wild and ignorant, I threw my lot
With that which beauty in each heart may bear
In silent testimony of all ruin.
What is beauty but an impure longing
For purity of form, a gazing in
Upon eternity contained by nothing?
There is no beauty without dignity.
That ravished land is no less beautiful.
Tepid abstract nouns come alive in me
When images of doom are bountiful.
There was a beauty I'll not know again.
There was a dignity that will not end.

Previous titles in the Carnegie Mellon Poetry Series

2001
Day Moon, Jon Anderson
The Origin of Green, T. Alan Broughton
Lovers in the Used World, Gillian Conoley
Quarters, James Harms
Mastodon, 80% Complete, Jonathan Johnson
The Deepest Part of the River, Mekeel McBride
Earthly, Michael McFee
Ten Thousand Good Mornings, James Reiss
The World's Last Night, Margot Schilpp
Sex Lives of the Poor and Obscure, David Schloss
Glacier Wine, Maura Stanton
Voyages in English, Dara Wier

2002
Keeping Time, Suzanne Cleary
Astronaut, Brian Henry
What It Wasn't, Laura Kasischke
Slow Risen Among the Smoke Trees, Elizabeth Kirschner
The Finger Bone, Kevin Prufer
Among the Musk Ox People, Mary Ruefle
The Late World, Arthur Smith

2003
Trouble, Mary Baine Campbell
A Place Made of Starlight, Peter Cooley
Taking Down the Angel, Jeff Friedman
Lives of Water, John Hoppenthaler
Imitation of Life, Allison Joseph
Except for One Obscene Brushstroke, Dzvinia Orlowsky
The Mastery Impulse, Ricardo Pau-Llosa
Casino of the Sun, Jerry Williams

2004
The Women Who Loved Elvis All Their Lives, Fleda Brown
The Chronic Liar Buys a Canary, Elizabeth Edwards

Freeways and Aqueducts, James Harms
Prague Winter, Richard Katrovas
Trains in Winter, Jay Meek
Tristimania, Mary Ruefle
Venus Examines Her Breast, Maureen Seaton
Various Orbits, Thom Ward

2005
Things I Can't Tell You, Michael Dennis Browne
Bent to the Earth, Blas Manuel De Luna
Blindsight, Carol Hamilton
Fallen from a Chariot, Kevin Prufer
Needlegrass, Dennis Sampson
Laws of My Nature, Margot Schilpp
Sleeping Woman, Herbert Scott
Renovation, Jeffrey Thomson

2006
Burn the Field, Amy Beeder
The Sadness of Others, Hayan Charara
A Grammar to Waking, Nancy Eimers
Dog Star Delicatessen: New and Selected Poems 1979–2006,
        Mekeel McBride
Shinemaster, Michael McFee
Eastern Mountain Time, Joyce Peseroff
Dragging the Lake, Robert Thomas

2007
Trick Pear, Suzanne Cleary
So I Will Till the Ground, Gregory Djanikian
Black Threads, Jeff Friedman
Drift and Pulse, Kathleen Halme
The Playhouse Near Dark, Elizabeth Holmes
On the Vanishing of Large Creatures, Susan Hutton
One Season Behind, Sarah Rosenblatt
Indeed I Was Pleased with the World, Mary Ruefle
The Situation, John Skoyles

2008
The Grace of Necessity, Samuel Green
After West, James Harms

Anticipate the Coming Reservoir, John Hoppenthaler
Convertible Night, Flurry of Stones, Dzvinia Orlowsky
Parable Hunter, Ricardo Pau-Llosa
The Book of Sleep, Eleanor Stanford

2009
Divine Margins, Peter Cooley
Cultural Studies, Kevin A. González
Dear Apocalypse, K. A. Hays
Warhol-o-rama, Peter Oresick
Cave of the Yellow Volkswagen, Maureen Seaton
Group Portrait from Hell, David Schloss
Birdwatching in Wartime, Jeffrey Thomson

2010
The Diminishing House, Nicky Beer
A World Remembered, T. Alan Broughton
Say Sand, Daniel Coudriet
Knock Knock, Heather Hartley
In the Land We Imagined Ourselves, Jonathan Johnson
Selected Early Poems: 1958-1983, Greg Kuzma
The Other Life: Selected Poems, Herbert Scott
Admission, Jerry Williams

2011
Having a Little Talk with Capital P Poetry, Jim Daniels
Oz, Nancy Eimers
Working in Flour, Jeff Friedman
Scorpio Rising: Selected Poems, Richard Katrovas
The Politics, Benjamin Paloff
Copperhead, Rachel Richardson

2012
Now Make an Altar, Amy Beeder
Still Some Cake, James Cummins
Comet Scar, James Harms
Early Creatures, Native Gods, K. A. Hays
That Was Oasis, Michael McFee
Blue Rust, Joseph Millar
Spitshine, Anne Marie Rooney
Civil Twilight, Margot Schilpp

2013
Oregon, Henry Carlile
Selvage, Donna Johnson
At the Autopsy of Vaslav Nijinksy, Bridget Lowe
Silvertone, Dzvinia Orlowsky
Fibonacci Batman: New & Selected Poems (1991-2011),
    Maureen Seaton
When We Were Cherished, Eve Shelnutt
The Fortunate Era, Arthur Smith
Birds of the Air, David Yezzi

2014
Night Bus to the Afterlife, Peter Cooley
Alexandria, Jasmine Bailey
Dear Gravity, Gregory Djanikian
Pretenders, Jeff Friedman
How I Went Red, Maggie Glover
All That Might Be Done, Samuel Green
Man, Ricardo Pau-Llosa
The Wingless, Cecilia Llompart

2015
The Octopus Game, Nicky Beer
The Voices, Michael Dennis Browne
Domestic Garden, John Hoppenthaler
We Mammals in Hospitable Times, Jynne Dilling Martin
And His Orchestra, Benjamin Paloff
Know Thyself, Joyce Peseroff
cadabra, Dan Rosenberg
The Long Haul, Vern Rutsala
Bartram's Garden, Eleanor Stanford

2016
Something Sinister, Hayan Charara
The Spokes of Venus, Rebecca Morgan Frank
Adult Swim, Heather Hartley
Swastika into Lotus, Richard Katrovas
The Nomenclature of Small Things, Lynn Pedersen
Hundred-Year Wave, Rachel Richardson